995

Practical Strategies for
Living with Dyslexia

of related interest

Dyslexia
How Would I Cope? 3rd edition
Michael Ryden
ISBN 1 85302 385 X

Asperger's Syndrome
A Guide for Parents and Professionals
Tony Attwood
Foreword by Lorna Wing
ISBN 1 85302 577 1

Marching to a Different Tune
Diary About an ADHD Boy
Jacky Fletcher
ISBN 1 85302 810 X

Helping Children with Dyspraxia
Maureen Boon
ISBN 1 85302 881 9

From Thoughts to Obsessions
Obsessive Compulsive Disorder in Children and Adolescents
Per Hove Thomsen
ISBN 1 85302 721 9

Attention Deficit/Hyperactivity Disorder
A Multidisciplinary Approach
Henryk Holowenko
ISBN 1 85302 741 3

The ADHD Handbook
A Guide for Parents and Professionals on Attention Deficit/Hyperactivity Disorder
Alison Munden and Jon Arcelus
ISBN 1 85302 756 1

Check-Mate
A Pocket-Size Guide to Everyday Spellings for Dyslexics
Alan O'Brien
ISBN 1 85302 165 2

Practical Strategies for Living with Dyslexia

Maria Chivers

Jessica Kingsley Publishers
London and Philadelphia

The right of Maria Chivers to be identified as author of this work has been asserted by her in accordance with the Copyright, Designs and Patents Act 1988.

First published in the United Kingdom in 2001 by
Jessica Kingsley Publishers Ltd,
116 Pentonville Road,
London N1 9JB,
England
and
325 Chestnut Street,
Philadelphia, PA 19106, USA.

www.jkp.com

Copyright © 2001 Maria Chivers

Library of Congress Cataloging in Publication Data
A CIP catalog record for this book is available from the Library of Congress

British Library Cataloguing in Publication Data
A CIP catalogue record for this book is available from the British Library

ISBN 1 85302 905 X

Printed and Bound in Great Britain by
Athenaeum Press, Gateshead, Tyne and Wear

This book is dedicated to my two sons Jeremy and Mark, who have been virtual guinea pigs for most of the methods and strategies described in this book – looking for a 'miracle cure'. It is also dedicated to the British Dyslexia Association for their help and assistance over the last decade.

Contents

Acknowledgements

I would like to express my thanks to the specialists who have kindly contributed to this book – Keith Holland, Colin Lane, Gail Saye and Chris Vickers – and to the British Dyslexia Association for their help over the years, for me personally and professionally.

Famous People with Dyslexia

You can see from this list that dyslexia is not a disability; it is having *different abilities*. It does not stop you getting on in life – often it is the opposite.

Hans Christian Andersen	Michael Barrymore
Dennis Bergkamp	Marlon Brando
Richard Branson	Cher
Agatha Christie	Winston Churchill
Margi Clark	Brian Connolly
Tom Cruise	Charles Darwin
Walt Disney	Albert Einstein
Whoopi Goldberg	Duncan Goodhew
Susan Hampshire	Carol Harrison
Goldie Hawn	Michael Heseltine
Jeremy Irons	Eddie Izzard
Lynda La Plante	Ruth Madoc
Steve Redgrave	Richard Rogers
Jackie Stewart	Anthea Turner
Leonardo da Vinci	Benjamin Zephaniah

Introduction

This book is for *you*. Whatever your interest in dyslexia either as a parent, teacher or other professional this information will be of great assistance.

My work at the Swindon Dyslexia Centre over the last ten years has included dealing with several thousand people who were desperately seeking the 'cure' for dyslexia but did not know what was available or where to get it. Over the last decade dyslexia has been under the scrutiny of many different specialists including optometrists, dieticians, linguists, audiologists, psychologists and other therapists. The result has been that there is a wealth of information available today.

This book contains different methods and strategies for treating dyslexia. Some you will know about, others you may have seen in the papers but do not know how they work. There are of course many different learning programmes and software packages available; I could not possibly include them all. After reading this book you will be in a better position to judge for yourself the merits of vitamin supplements, coloured glasses, exercises and audiotapes, to name but a few. You may find some of the methods appear a little unorthodox, but believe me it is worth keeping an open mind.

If I do not achieve anything else, I hope I will convince you of the importance of having children assessed when they are still very young in order that appropriate help can be sought. Early identification is the key to happy and contented children.

Note: I have used 'he' throughout the book as the majority of people with dyslexia are male and for ease of reading.

CHAPTER I

What are Dyslexia and Dyscalculia?

Dyslexia

Dyslexia affects 4 per cent of the population. Problems can show themselves in reading, writing, number work, short-term memory, hand control and visual processing. Timekeeping, sense of direction and interpersonal skills can also be affected. These difficulties often result in great frustration, bearing in mind that dyslexics are often of high or above-average intelligence.

Dyslexia affects more males than females. Many of these children are extremely bright in lots of ways, always talking and asking questions; yet they do not seem to reach their full potential in the academic field. One of the best definitions of dyslexia I have heard is by Dr J. E. Cullis: 'Dyslexia means having difficulty with words in reading, spelling and writing – *in spite of* having normal intelligence and ability.'

The following is a checklist for dyslexia. However, when children start school, they may make several of the mistakes listed below. It is only if these symptoms continue beyond the time that the average child has grown out of them that they may indicate dyslexia and advice should be sought.

Dyslexia Checklist
READING AND SPELLING

When your child reads and spells, does he frequently:

- confuse letters that look similar: d – b, u – n, m – n
- confuse letters that sound the same: v, f, th
- reverse words: was – saw, now – won
- transpose letters: left – felt, help – hepl
- read a word correctly and then, further down the page, read it wrongly
- change words around: the cat sat on the mat (the mat sat on the cat)
- confuse small words: of, for, from
- have difficulty in keeping the correct place
- read correctly without understanding what he is reading?

WRITING

Even after frequent instruction does he still:

- not know whether to use his right or left hand
- leave out capital letters or use them in the wrong places
- forget to dot i's and cross t's
- form letters and numbers badly
- fail to use margins
- slope his writing down the page
- use punctuation and paragraphs in the wrong places?

OTHER INDICATORS

- late developer

- other members of the family with similar difficulties

- easily distracted and poor concentration

- auditory difficulties

- confusion between: left/right, east/west, up/down, over/under

- sequencing difficulties: alphabet, nursery rhymes, months of the year, numbers in tables

- holds pen too tightly

- confusion with mathematical symbols (plus/minus, etc.)

- problems telling the time

- problems with tying shoelaces

- mixed laterality (i.e. uses either right or left hand or eye, in writing and other tasks)

- particular difficulty copying from a blackboard

- short-term memory problems relating to printed words and instructions

- inability to follow more than one instruction at a time

- inability to use a dictionary or telephone directory

Dyscalculia

Dyscalculia is a specific learning difficulty in mathematics. Like dyslexia, dyscalculia can be caused by a visual perceptual deficit. Dyscalculia refers specifically to the inability to perform operations in maths or arithmetic. Along with dyslexia, the extent to which you can be affected varies tremendously in each individual. And like dyslexia, where there is no single set of signs that characterises all dyslexics, there is no one symtom of dyscalculia.

Dyscalculia Checklist

When your child attempts maths problems does he frequently have difficulties with:

- recognising numbers
- understanding the signs: +, −, / and x
- adding numbers
- subtracting numbers
- the words 'plus', 'add', 'add together'
- the sequence of numbers − reversing numbers (e.g. 15 becomes 51) or transposing numbers (e.g. 364 becomes 634)
- multiplication tables
- mental arithmetic
- telling the time
- following instructions?

Students may have difficulties with mathematics, calculations and learning number facts such as multiplication tables. It is important that children start developing skills with sequencing, space organisation, deduction and strategy.

Around 60 per cent of dyslexics have difficulties with dyscalculia; yet although this has been well documented in the United States, it is still practically unheard of in Britain.

CHAPTER 2

Identifying Dyslexia

Many children experiencing difficulties at school do not have their problems identified until the child starts to fail. Some children are simply put down as lazy or as late developers. A child's educational needs should be assessed and diagnosed as early as possible.

If your child is giving some cause for concern, or if he appears to be brighter than his achievements, you can arrange for a private dyslexic assessment. It is important to know where he is in his reading and spelling and that his strengths are identified and developed so he achieves success in some areas. Years ago, tests were only carried out after a child had reached seven years of age, or in many cases even later. These days there is a variety of tests available from four years of age. Some of these tests do not require a child to read or write – they simply 'play' with a computer.

Tests vary in duration from twenty minutes to four hours. The shorter test has a place as it can quickly and easily establish whether there is a problem, and usually what is causing it. The longer tests can take up to four hours and give a thorough background, including an intelligence quotient (IQ). The most comprehensive of all is the educational psychologist's report. This is usually regarded as the Rolls Royce of tests.

All these tests give a good indication of the child's strengths as well as his weaknesses. They also show where the child is at the moment and what he is capable of performing. It is no good expecting a child to be top of the class if he is not able to reach that level, nor is it right that we should accept a child's under-performing if he is capable of doing better.

There are many different tests and assessments available today and I could not attempt to write about them all. I have listed the ones that I have used and that are well known in the field of dyslexia. The cost of the tests and assessments can range from £30 to £500.

• Aston Index Assessment.	5–14 years
• Cognitive Profiling System (CoPS) *	4–8 years
• Dyslexia Early Screening Test (DEST)	4:6–6:5 years
• Dyslexia Screening Test (DST)	6:6–16:5 years
• Dyslexia Adult Screening Test (DAST)	16:6 years +
• Educational Psychologist Report	Any age
• Lucid Assessment System for Schools (LASS)*	11–15 years
• Phonological Assessment Battery (PhAB)	6–14:11

*The Cognitive Profiling System (CoPS) and Lucid Assessment System for Schools (LASS) are fully computerised.

Further information from NfER-Nelson (see 'Useful Addresses' p.000).

Aston Index Assessment

The Aston Index is a test for screening and diagnosis of language difficulties for children from five to 14 years of age. It consists of 17 subtests and will indicate the nature of a child's learning potential for literacy. The subtest scores yield a profile, from which a teacher can perceive the levels of readiness for learning, and which skills and abilities will need special help in teaching. It can give one an indication of the child's potential.

Further information from LDA Living & Learning (See 'Useful Addresses' p.000).

Cognitive Profiling System (CoPS)

COPS is a unique computer program for the assessment of dyslexia and other learning difficulties for children from four to eight years of age. CoPS is a major breakthrough in the identification and assessment of dyslexia and other special educational needs, which now meets statutory requirements within schools. (A useful guide to statutory requirements is the Department for Education's (1994) Code of Practice on the Identification and Assessment of Special Educational Needs.)

CoPS identifies the cognitive abilities that underpin learning for all children. It has proved useful in identifying dyslexia and other special educational needs. CoPS can be administered by teachers and non-teaching assistants and is fun for children to use. Not only is it used for early diagnosis but it can be used as a screening test on school entry to identify the learning needs of all children.

All this information can be applied in formulating Individual Education Plans (IEPs) and is valuable when deliberating whether to request a formal assessment by an educational psychologist.

A licence to use the CoPS program can be bought by schools and educational professionals. This costs between £62 and £290, according to size of institution and duration of licence. A demonstration disk is available free. Further information may be sought from Lucid Research Ltd (see 'Useful Addresses' p.96).

Dyslexia Screening Tests

Dyslexia Early Screening Test and Dyslexia Screening Test

The Dyslexia Early Screening Test (DEST) is for children from 4:6 to 6:5 years and the Dyslexia Screening Test (DST) is for children from 6:6 to 16:5 years of age. They provide a profile of strengths and weaknesses, which can form an integral part of an initial identification procedure. It can also be used in guiding the formation of an IEP. The tests are designed to pick out children who are at risk of reading failure early enough to allow them to be given extra support. As the main purpose of these tests is to identify children who are in need of further support, it is vital to take appropriate action having administered the tests.

Each of these kits can be purchased for £71.00 ex VAT. Further information is available from Pyschological Corporation (see 'Useful Addresses' p.97).

Dyslexia Adult Screening Test

The Dyslexia Adult Screening Test (DAST) is intended as a screening instrument for students from 16:6 years of age. The DAST forms a valuable first step in deciding whether to request a further full assessment by a qualified psychologist. It also provides a profile of strengths and weaknesses that can be used to guide the development of support within the workplace or educational institute. The purpose of the DAST is to identify students who are in need of further support. Consequently it is vital to take appropriate action having administered the DAST. The DAST provides key information for subsequent action. This may be included in a programme for adults with special educational needs, or used as the basis for possible referral for examination concessions.

The complete kit can be purchased for £114.50 ex VAT. Further information is avaliable from Psychological Corporation (see 'Useful Addresses' p.97).

Educational Psychologist Report

An educational psychologist's report is the most comprehensive of all the tests available and checks the student's intelligence quotient (IQ). This is necessary to ensure that the student is not under-performing; it would be unfair if a student with a low IQ were being pushed beyond his capabilities. An educational psychologist assesses a student to see the areas of strengths as well as weaknesses. After testing, a detailed report will indicate the areas in which the student will gain most help. This report can then be used to design an IEP for the student at school.

Educational psychologists are available free through many schools, colleges and universities. However, they will only be consulted if the school feels there is a long-term problem and this may take a considerable time to arrange. You can see an educational psychologist privately in order to get the child's needs established quickly.

For further information contact the Association of Educational Psychologists (see 'Useful Addresses' p.94).

Lucid Assessment System for Schools

This is a unique computer program for the assessment of dyslexia and other learning difficulties for children from 11 to 15 years of age.

Like CoPS, Lucid Assessment System for Schools (LASS) is a major breakthrough in the identification and assessment of dyslexia and other special educational needs which now meets statutory requirements within schools (see Department for Education 1994). LASS measures cognitive, literacy and intellectual abilities. A profile of phonic/phonological skills, memory, reading, spelling and reasoning can be produced for all children to see if they are fulfilling their potential. LASS can be self-administered by students and is fun to use for children of all abilities. Its use is proven in the identification of dyslexia and other special educational needs. The information the assessment provides can be used in formulating IEPs and is valuable when deliberating whether to request a formal assessment by an educational psychologist.

A licence to use the LASS program can be bought by schools or educational professionals. This costs between £75 and £250, according to size of institution and duration of licence. A demonstration disk is available free. Further information is avaliable from Lucid Research Ltd (see 'Useful Addresses' p.96).

Phonological Assessment Battery

The Phonological Assessment Battery (PhAB) is used for children from 6 to 14:11 years of age. Awareness of and sensitivity to the sounds in language are acknowledged to be important factors in reading ability. In order to help those who have difficulties in this key area, The Phonological Assessment Battery aims to identify phonologically based specific learning difficulties by the assessment of six different abilities, namely:

- alliteration/alliteration with pictures

- naming speed

- rhyme

- spoonerisms

- fluency

- non-word reading.

Summary

As you can see there is a wide range of tests available for identifying dyslexia. Whichever one you choose, please remember that it is imperative to do so early. Many parents say that they knew there was something wrong at a very early age, often when the child started playgroup or nursery.

CHAPTER 3

What Causes Dyslexia?

Dyslexia was identified over a century ago, yet little was known about its causes until interest in the condition began to grow in the early 1970s. It was about this time that the British Dyslexia Association (BDA) was formed.

One of the earlier assumptions used to be that dyslexia was a middle class disease. This came about because people in the middle income bracket could afford to have their children tested for dyslexia, while people from disadvantaged backgrounds were often simply put down as slow or backward. Thankfully, these assumptions no longer exist due to a great deal of research being carried out into the causes of dyslexia.

You can see from the following research, published in the BDA Bulletin in October 1999 that it is now widely accepted that the dyslexic brain is different.

Two major pieces or research hit the headline last summer. The first, from Southern Illinois University, claimed that by monitoring the responses of a new-born infant to sounds, it was possible to tell whether the child would grow up to be dyslexic.

The researchers said they accurately picked out 22 of the 24 dyslexics among 186 children whose brain waves were monitored 36 hours after birth.

Speech and non-speech sounds were played, while scientists monitored the sex and speed of the new-born's brainwave responses, through electrodes attached to the babies' scalps.

Every two years until they were eight, the children then sat IQ and comprehension tests. By the age of eight, the dyslexic youngsters could then be identified.

The method was not foolproof, however – five out of 24 readers with a similar brain wave pattern to the dyslexics were found to have normal reading skills by their eighth birthdays.

The BDA response was to welcome these findings cautiously, stressing that the interesting new research further endorsed the fact that the dyslexic brain is different, and emphasising a special focus on language skills at a young age to help dyslexic children when they start matching letters to sounds as they begin reading.

In the first week of September, a report was published about the finding of a gene location for dyslexia by an international team of scientists. The report was based on studies of a large Norwegian family, many of whom experienced reading and writing difficulties.

The scientists found that 11 family members shared an oddity in a small region of chromosome 2, one of 23 pairs of chromosomes found in every human cell.

The gene joins another which has been identified by British researchers on chromosome 6, and two others on chromosomes 1 and 15, building up a picture of dyslexia as a syndrome caused by several environmental and inherited factors.

The BDA stressed that there has always been plentiful anecdotal evidence suggesting dyslexia ran in families – many adults only discover their own problems when their children's difficulties are identified – and welcomed the suggestion that the areas of the brain responsible for language development are relatively plastic in the early years of life.

It is now indisputable that dyslexia is a neurological condition whose symptoms are most often demonstrated with difficulties in reading, writing, spelling and sometimes numeracy.

I believe that one of the major advances in dyslexia will be made in the area of genetics and it may not be too long before babies are tested at birth, thereby enabling help to be given at a very early age.

CHAPTER 4

Vision

Visual problems are one of the most common causes of disability in the world. In Britain nearly one million people are blind or partially sighted, and over 20,000 of these are children.

Most parents visit their doctor and dentist regularly, yet many of them still do not appreciate the necessity of taking their children to an optician. The Optical Information Council has estimated that one child in five may have undetected visual problems. Regular eye tests using new techniques may prevent children with learning difficulties from being labelled 'problem children' and would enable children to be identified at a much earlier age. It is imperative that these tests are carried out before the child starts to fail, as the damage caused to their self-esteem is very difficult to restore.

There have been enormous amounts of research over the last decade and many major advances in the orthoptic field, with new ideas and testing available. Tests and visual aids available include:

- standard and specialist eye tests
- Irlen syndrome tests
- Intuitive Colorimeter
- Cerium overlays
- ChromaGen Lenses

- Dunlop Test
- Visual Tracking Magnifier (VTM).

Eye Tests

A simple eye test is available at your local opticians and can quickly reveal whether there are difficulties with vision which could be causing problems in reading and writing. This test should always be carried out before going on to more specialist testing.

Specialist Eye Tests

Many children with learning difficulties need to have specialist eye tests. Some of these tests can be carried out at your local opticians or at specialist eye clinics or other medical centres. It is important that people who have a primary interest in special needs carry out these tests.

Headlines like 'Experts hail cure for child dyslexia' and 'A miracle cure' have appeared in most national newspapers over the last few years. And they have all been talking about the wonderful success being achieved by scores of dyslexic students. The remarkable achievements have occurred after being prescribed vision training or tinted glasses.

Tinted Glasses and Coloured Overlays

Irlen Syndrome

It was in 1983 that an American psychologist, Helen Irlen, discovered a perceptual problem caused by light sensitivity. Irlen found that some students benefited from the use of coloured overlays. The overlays seemed to work by filtering out light that caused distortions to print. The problems appeared to be worse with black print on white paper. Students reported problems with eyestrain, migraine, etc., and found it difficult to judge heights, distances and speeds. Once the overlays were used students appeared to read better.

Irlen syndrome is thought to affect about 50 per cent of students with specific learning difficulties, such as dyslexia.

You may benefit from tinted glasses or lenses if when reading you find:

- letters merging together
- letters appearing in the wrong order
- twirling letters
- fuzzy words
- words jumping about
- words appearing as a jumbled puzzle
- words appearing faded.

Associated problems include difficulties in reading and keeping your place and excessive rubbing and blinking of eyes.

Crium Overlays

The original overlays were designed by Professor Arnold Willains to be used as a preliminary test before using the Colorimeter. They were poduced in conjunction with the Institute of Optometry where a lot of the development work was done with Dr. Bruce Evans, an optometrist who is an expert in this area.

The Institute of Optometry is a registered charity and relies on income from the overlays to continue working with people who have Specific Learning Difficulties.

If you suspect someone may have a problem, Cerium Overlays are a logical and inexpensive first step towards assessment.

A quick and simple screening test uses clear coloured plastic sheets that are placed over written work. They work by reducing the perceptual distortions of text. When the overlays are placed over the text many students say 'the words have stopped jumping about'. Research indicates that a large majority of students read more quickly and better using the overlays.

The overlays are available in a wide range of colours and students should try them to see which one is the most comfortable. If after approximately four weeks the student feels the overlay is helping, it is recommended to have a full test at the opticians using the Intuitive Colorimeter.

The Cerium Overlays and Screening Kit can be purchased through Cerium Visual Technologies (see 'Useful Addresses' p.000).

Richard – 10 years

'A Miracle Cure' – this was what one family said about the amazing success of their young son.

Concerned with Richard's poor performance at school and his reading age of just six years, Richard's parents brought him to the Swindon Dyslexia Centre for a Dyslexia Screening Test to ascertain what was causing his reading and writing problems. The results proved what his parents already knew – he could barely read or spell and his writing was illegible. The teacher knew immediately that there was something else wrong. She carried out the Cerium Coloured Overlay test and Richard said: 'The words have all jumped back in the right place. I can read them now.' He went on to read without assistance.

After the opticians carried out a full examination using the Intuitive Colorimeter he was prescribed tinted lenses. He is continuing to make excellent progress and his parents feel that it was nothing short of miraculous.

Intuitive Colorimeter

The Intuitive Colorimeter uses up to 7000 tints to measure exactly which colour helps individual students.

Scientists do not know exactly how this technique works but they believe that the area in the brain that controls vision is very sensitive and some text may overexcite the colour neurones resulting in text being distorted. It appears that the coloured lenses filter out light, helping to correct the problem.

Students who appear to benefit most from these lenses are those who find that words and letters tend to be jumbled up, move around, wobble and appear in the wrong order. Some students have most of the following symptoms while others may only have one. Often, students do not realise it is a problem as they have always seen writing in the same way. Research has shown that if a child uses coloured overlays his reading speed increases and he has fewer headaches.

The full screening test using the Intuitive Colorimeter is not available on the National Health Service and can only be arranged through participating optometrists. (List available from Cerium Visual Technologies – see 'Useful Addresses').

ChromaGen Lenses

ChromaGen lenses were developed at the Corneal Laser Centre for colour blindness at Clattersbridge Hospital, Wirral. It was purely by accident that a researcher, David Harris, noticed that after he had examined a patient, the patient said that for the first time 'the words have gone straight'. It was this remark that led to further research into the effect of the lenses on dyslexia.

The ChromaGen lens is similar to ordinary soft contact lenses, but has a tiny speck of colour that is almost invisible. The eyes have to be treated individually, resulting in a different colour spot for each eye. Scientists still do not know exactly how these lenses work, but it appears that the two colours filter light entering the eyes, which helps to correct the problem. Harris has run several studies which have all shown that the lenses improve the speed and reading ability of people with dyslexia.

Ultralase (formerly known as the Corneal Laser Centre) who supply ChronaGen lenses say that the system produces a highly significant effect, with an average increase in overall reading speed of 24 per cent. The ChromaGen system of lenses has been awarded

'Millennium Product' status by the Design Council to recognise forward thinking, challenging, creative and innovative products.

For further information on ChromaGen lenses contact Ultralase (see 'Useful Addresses' p.93).

Dunlop Test

The Dunlop Test was designed in 1971 by Patricia Dunlop, an orthoptist, to ascertain whether a child has a fixed 'reference eye'. If the reference eye is not established this could lead to learning difficulties with:

- reading

- writing

- number work

- close work.

If your child has an eye problem he may be referred to an eye clinic. An orthoptist will assess his binocular vision to see how his eyes work together and to make sure one eye is dominant. Children usually have a fixed reference eye by the time they are seven. If treatment is necessary glasses with one side frosted or eye exercises may be prescribed.

This test is available on the National Health Service; your doctor will be able to refer you to your nearest orthoptics department.

Visual Tracking Magnifier

A new optical device, which is claimed will help millions in the treatment of reading difficulties such as dyslexia, was awarded 'Millennium Product' status by the Design Council in 1999. Called the Visual Tracking Magnifier (VTM) the new device is the result of many years' research by Ian Jordan, who is well known for his pioneering work in designing equipment that can effectively measure and treat visual dyslexia.

Many visual dyslexia sufferers are confused by 'pattern glare', which causes whole blocks of text to merge and swim above the page to make reading extremely difficult. Jordan has combated this problem by creating a device that modifies the way the reader's eyes approach the print.

The VTM sits on a page and can be easily tracked backwards and forwards across the text. It consists of a high-powered magnifying glass, with a central viewing strip about one centimetre wide. Above and below this strip are two semicircular transparent patterned areas that remove any distortion of the surrounding text. As a result, a high proportion of visual dyslexics can read text much more easily.

Jordan believes the greatest benefit from the new device will be found in school classrooms, where the VTM will help an estimated 10 to 15 per cent of pupils in an average class, but with even greater numbers benefiting in lower achievement groups.

The Visual Tracking Magnifier is available at £38.00 (plus £1.00 p&p) from Edward Marcus Ltd (see 'Useful Addresses').

Vision and Learning Difficulties
by Keith Holland

The role of vision problems in children with learning difficulties has varied in popularity over the last 20 years, but has recently come to the fore again with the development of coloured contact lenses for the treatment of dyslexia. However, whilst this development has captured journalistic imagination, there are several other areas that are in fact of greater importance, and affect far more children. Any parent looking for help for their child with a learning difficulty should ensure that they have checked out the possibility of vision problems at an early stage.

Several recent studies have suggested that as many as 80 per cent of dyslexic children have unresolved eye problems contributing to their reading and spelling difficulties – even though they may see well and pass simple vision screening tests such as those carried out in schools. So what are these eye problems, and what can you do about them?

To read effortlessly, the eyes need to be able to perform four functions. First, they must see well, so that the brain receives a clear image. Surprisingly, this is not as critical as it may seem, for we are able to work with quite blurred images. However, good visual acuity and no more than a small degree of refractive error are desirable.

Second, the eyes must team together well, so that both are directed to the same point. Breakdown in this can ultimately lead to a squint, but this rarely affects reading as the brain will normally have developed compensatory strategies to overcome the misalignment of the eyes. It is where there is a small and intermittent breakdown that the biggest problems arise – and these are the hardest types of misalignment to pick up on screening tests. Typically, the sufferer will be aware of print moving about on the page, seeming to shimmer, and possibly appearing splotchy. He may also be more aware of the white spaces between words, and find that his 'span of regard' has reduced from six to nine letters to as little as two letters, in turn leading to a need for more scanning eye movements.

Third, the eyes must focus well. Where there is a reduction in focusing (known as accommodative insufficiency) it may not be possible to keep a near image clear, and a loss of concentration may again be seen. This is probably the least common of the main visual factors affecting reading, and is most often secondary to convergence difficulties.

Fourth, there must be good eye-movement skills. A deficiency here, commonly though incorrectly called tracking difficulty, affects the ability to move the eyes in a controlled and sequential manner along a line, and to switch from the end of one line to the start of another. Loss of place occurs, and there is a need to use a finger or marker to help prevent this. So much effort may be put into maintaining position that there is a tendency to lose the meaning of what has been read. Comprehension suffers, and the enjoyment and understanding that should accompany reading is no longer possible.

In all of these situations the result is an increase in the attentional demands on control, to the detriment of attention to the subject matter. As soon as the visual factors are stabilised, increased attention to the subject matter arises. As this can sometimes be achieved almost instantly through the judicious use of glasses, it is especially important that eyes are carefully investigated for signs of such difficulties.

Just as orthodontics is a specialism within dentistry, so the investigation of visual factors affecting reading is fast becoming a specialism within optometry. It is wise to seek personal recommendation to an appropriate professional for investigation. One useful source of information is the British Association of Behaviour Optometrists, which maintains a register of suitably trained optometrists in the field. Treatment may take the form of glasses for reading, or of individually planned exercise programmes that rely on developing the required skills in a manner that prevents the individual creating compensatory strategies. Sometimes this will involve visiting a practice regularly for in-house work, whilst for others the exercises may be carried out at home. Often more general signs of difficulty are seen, such as travel sickness or problems with co-ordination and sport, and suitable programmes can help in both of these areas.

Recently research has highlighted the existence of two channels for transporting information in the brain – known as the 'Parvo' and 'Magno' channels. It would seem that many dyslexics have difficulty in integrating the two systems effectively. Whilst most of this work is still very much in the laboratory, there is promise for new and exciting ways to help dyslexics, and for a better understanding of the underlying conditions that affect so many. The development of coloured lens therapies, such as the Irlen system, the Intuitive Colorimeter system, and the ChromoGen coloured filter system are all early attempts to stabilise the symptoms of visual difficulty, and would appear to alter the relationship between these two channels. Currently however, all of these systems appear to work merely by relieving symptoms, and not by changing any underlying mechanism.

In the 1980s, and again in the last 12 months, interest has been aroused in the concept of unstable eye dominance as a cause of some reading difficulties. Whilst the latest work is still very new and has not yet been evaluated by other researchers, there is certainly evidence that some dyslexics do not have well-developed patterns of dominance, and that this affects their ability to scan in a controlled left to right direction. Such individuals make more directional errors, often reversing letters such as b and d, and experiencing difficulty with number sequences. Current methods of treating these problems include over-learning and the use of movement therapies to develop the underlying dominance patterns – both are time consuming but effective, and should not be ruled out.

Typical signs and symptoms that may suggest a vision-related learning difficulty:

- complaints of blurred print when reading – possibly over a prolonged period

- transient double vision at near work – words may be described as 'wobbling about', changing from black to grey and back, or having shadows

- difficulty keeping place or line – a need for a marker is classic of scanning difficulties

- problems remembering what has been read – reduced comprehension suggests increased attention is needed for visual control

- eyestrain, headaches or fatigue with close work – all suggest that excessive effort is required, and all lead to reduced efficiency.

In this short piece the significance of vision problems in learning has been identified. Ideas on what to look for, as well as what can be done, have been put forward. The reader who would like more information and has access to the internet should search some of the relevant websites, including a portal site of the author's that gives access to many other sites of interest (see p.89).

Summary

Each of these tests and methods uses a slightly different way of identifying and correcting vision problems. However, many behavioural optometrists believe that although coloured lenses and glasses may help in the short term, they do not *correct* the underlying problem, and that eye problems will not go away without children receiving vision training. Many parents have seen immediate benefits just from their child wearing tinted lenses or glasses. It is up to parents to decide whether the use of such glasses should be the sole treatment or to err on the side of caution and visit a behaviour optometrist as well.

As some students see such dramatic results with these methods, it may be that in the next few years we will see the tests described in this chapter carried out along with the standard eye tests.

CHAPTER 5

Hearing

In Britain over eight million people suffer from hearing loss and over 25,000 of these are children. Deafness is often associated with older people. But many are born partially or profoundly deaf, while others become so after an illness. One million children (0–8 years) will experience temporary deafness caused by glue ear.

It has been shown that many young children with learning difficulties have hearing problems, some permanent but many temporary, such as glue ear. As many teaching methods rely on the use of phonics, these hearing problems cause children to hear muffled sounds, and confuse, for instance, 'b' and 'd'.

If a child cannot hear properly this may lead to literacy problems and there may be a simple remedy which can correct the problem quickly and easily. Wax in the ear canal is the most common problem. Wax is made naturally in the ear, but it can become a problem if excessive amounts are produced. It normally forms into small beads, mixes with dust and dead skin and falls out of the ear. This cleaning mechanism works well for most people and does not need help with cotton-tipped sticks or fingers – pushing things into the ear causes more wax and can push the wax firmly down into the drum resulting in pain and deafness. Some people make abnormal amounts of wax and may have to have it removed by a doctor or nurse.

Glue Ear

This is a common condition in childhood. The Eustachian tube (which drains and ventilates the middle ear) can become obstructed by mucus. Air cannot then enter the middle ear, and the cavity fills with fluid. The eardrum becomes dark looking. As time goes on the fluid becomes thicker until it has the consistency of thick glue. Often the only sign is deafness and children's schooling may suffer and behaviour may deteriorate.

In a lot of cases it will clear up by itself but in severe cases treatment will involve a simple operation, usually under anaesthetic. The problem usually disappears at puberty, and most children with glue ear do not need treatment after this time. Hearing is usually restored to normal.

Often the only sign of glue ear in the very young child is when he fails to start talking properly. However, these problems are often picked up when the child has a hearing test at six months and again just before starting school. If glue ear is not treated, these children may continue to have problems with talking, reading and writing.

There are several different ear tests available. Therefore, it is important to go back to your doctor or health visitor and ask for another check-up if you feel there may still be a problem.

Fast ForWord

Scientific Learning is a company founded to sell a computer game – Fast ForWord – intended to improve the hearing of children with language problems. Fast ForWord works on the principle that some children with language problems do not hear sounds correctly. It helps to improve phoneme recognition by accentuating each sound – as mothers do when they use baby talk.

Fast ForWord is a CD-ROM and internet-based training pro-gramme. It has been shown to improve phonological awareness, including auditory processing speed and working memory. The programme consists of regular daily training sessions for 20 minutes at a time.

For further information on Fast ForWord contact Scientific Learning (see 'Useful Addresses').

Aural–Read–Respond–Oral–Write (ARROW)
by Dr Colin Lane
The Improvement of Listening, Reading and Spelling Skills of Dyslexic Students

It is very important to realise that differences exist between hearing (a faculty) and listening (a pattern of behaviour).

HEARING

Hearing is a physiological state which depends upon an intact outer, middle and inner ear hearing system. In the outer ear system, sound is carried through the ear canal to the eardrum. At the eardrum the sound is conducted into the middle ear system through a series of bones. These in turn send sound into the inner ear system. In the inner ear system, the sound is changed into electrical impulses before being sent to the brain via the auditory nerve.

Any defect in either of the outer, middle or inner ear systems can cause hearing loss. This hearing loss can in turn cause problems in speech, communication and literacy skills. Most deaf school leavers have experienced severe problems in reading and spelling despite having the normal range of intelligence.

Fortunately, the greater proportion of dyslexic children have an intact hearing system. However, despite having normal hearing, they usually have other auditory problems.

LISTENING

Listening, here defined as auditory attention, does not require a fully intact hearing system. Listening is an acquired skill. Listening varies from child to child among the normally hearing or hearing-impaired populations.

There is strong evidence to show that there are normally hearing students of all ages and abilities who experience severe problems when listening to speech in background noise. These auditory problems have the most significant effect upon their progress in reading and spelling.

Listening involves focusing and maintaining auditory attention. The listener needs to select the spoken word and then reject any irrelevant input such as background noise. Some mature motivated students maintain auditory attention for 45 minutes or more. In younger or easily distracted children such attention may only be a few minutes. There are many cases of children with reading and spelling difficulties experiencing severe auditory attention problems. Auditory attention is trainable.

The ARROW Technique

Young children learn better by listening to themselves and indeed prefer to listen to their own voices. The child's own voice, heard within the head, is that which is universally applied in memory tasks and for internal thought. A technique called ARROW has been developed from the use of the self-voice. ARROW is an acronym for Aural–Read–Respond–Oral–Write. The student listens to the tutor's voice through headsets and repeats what is heard. At the same time, the student reads text. The recording of the student's self-voice then forms the basis of the ARROW work. This work requires the student to take down dictation from passages of information, and precision spellings. The student checks the accuracy of the work undertaken.

ARROW programmes are centred on national curriculum requirements. When used in further education colleges, vocational and other curriculum work may be used.

The ARROW programme recognises the strong need for all reading and spelling work to be set within the student's ability level. Differentiation is therefore a cornerstone of the system together with the importance of the working short-term memory. Precision spellings are set within word families, frequently used words and similar sounding words having a dissimilar letter pattern. The ARROW tutor quickly establishes a starting level with a student on the programme. The tutor next helps the student make as near perfect a recording of the self-voice as possible whilst ensuring that the student remains on task.

The ARROW system is so flexible that ARROW training for students can be given within a week or spread over several weeks according to timetable and curriculum requirements. Students can work on their own or within groups.

A special audiocassette recorder is used to make recordings of the student's voice. An ordinary cassette player can be used when the student is listening to the tape. The ARROW approach is now being used on CD-ROM.

RESULTS

The ARROW self-voice technique can make a swift and dramatic impact on the listening, auditory processing and literacy skills of dyslexic students. Trained ARROW teachers and assistants are achieving up to eight months' progress in reading and seven months' progress in spelling within a total of two hours' one-to-one tuition. This tuition time can be split up as necessary. The students are required to work a further four hours, a little at a time, on their own, in order to complete a programme. Some teachers are reporting up to two or even three years' progress following a series of two or three short interventions.

Students quickly learn how to attend more effectively. Some students with attention problems can improve their listening in background noise up to and beyond the level of an adequate listener. In addition to the literacy and listening improvements other learning skills improve. Teachers report that students' self-esteem rises, as does the quality of their handwriting and their general classroom performance.

ARROW CENTRES

ARROW help is available for students through mainstream education. Where students cannot access these facilities ARROW provision also operates within specialist ARROW Centres. These centres can be at schools or colleges already using ARROW, but they also offer help to outside students. In addition, tutors operating from selected sites or operating from their own premises can provide help. Students attending ARROW Centres usually attend on a short once-weekly lesson for five or six weeks or undertake distance learning programmes.

ARROW TUTOR TRAINING

ARROW tutor training programmes operate on a regional basis. The ARROW programme has received national accreditation as an Advanced BTEC Award for ARROW Tutors. The training programme is essentially practical. During the course, trainee tutors attend a regionally based ARROW Centre for four separate days. The remaining part of the programme requires tutors to use the technique with their students. A report is submitted at the end of the third term of the programme. The course is open to professionals in education and health. In some cases, parents have been trained to work with their children.

Training courses are available for children and teachers.

For further information, please contact ARROW (see Useful Addresses' p.93).

Summary

If your child cannot hear properly it stands to reason that he may not be able to hear what is being said, especially if he sits at the back of the classroom. Ensure that a full ear test has been carried out and if necessary ask for a second opinion.

The ARROW Trust is well known and respected internationally as the leader in the field of reading, spelling, speaking and listening skills and has helped many thousands of children over the years.

CHAPTER 6

Development

There is a school of thought that many specific learning difficulties are due to developmental disorders. This does not mean that a child has been damaged but that certain early developmental reflexes have not fully matured. These reflexes normally develop spontaneously during a child's early years. Poor reflexes may lead to poor co-ordination and motor control.

Brain Gym

Brain Gym is part of the educational kinesiology process. It grew out of clinical studies started in 1969 by Dr Paul Dennison, an educational therapist. Dennison's research led him to the study of kinesiology – the science of body movement and the relationship of muscles and posture to brain function. For example a baby crawling develops connections between right and left hemispheres of the brain. Dennison looked at these innate movements and adapted them into a highly efficient system called Brain Gym.

It is claimed that Brain Gym can help students with dyslexia and dyspraxia by improving reading, writing, co-ordination and concentration.

For further information contact the Educational Kinesiology Foundation (see 'Useful Addresses').

Brain Injury Rehabilitation and Development

In 1982 David McGlown, a developmental psychologist, started the Centre for Brain Injury Rehabilitation and Development (BIRD). McGlown believes that children with poor motor skills and co-ordination have not developed mature reflexes. It is accepted that many dyslexic students have poor motor skills.

The BIRD Centre in Ipswich assesses students using a full physical test, where their responses, reflexes and co-ordination are tested. An individual exercise programme is designed for students to do at home each day. These exercises, whilst subtle and precise, help the immature reflexes to develop fully.

Neuro-Developmental Delay
by Gail Saye

Most specific learning difficulties are developmental disorders. This does not mean that there is damage but only that certain early developmental stages have not been perfected before going on to the next stage. A bit like the child who cannot get the hang of long division because he hasn't fully learned how to do short division – in other words he's not ready for it. This has become known as Neuro-Developmental Delay (NDD).

Neuro-developmental therapy can help children with the following difficulties:

- writing difficulties

- maths and spatial problems

- delayed speech

- school phobia

- immature behaviour

- dyslexia

- co-ordination problems

- clumsiness

- balance problems

- language disorders

- hypersensitivity

- dyspraxia.

We lay the foundations for all later development before our second birthday. We build a strong central nervous system that connects the brain and body, forging pathways that will carry the brain's messages to every part of us. We achieve this through repetitive movement dictated by our reflexes (automatic movements). When one skill has been perfected the reflex disappears to be replaced by another until we have worked through the whole repertoire. This developmental process is very orderly – the stages take place at the same time and in the same order for every baby.

Some Difficulties Caused by NDD

If there is a 'hiccup' in early development and these movements are not completely worked through, the central nervous system will be immature and all these processes, instead of running smoothly and automatically, will also be immature and we have to work hard to compensate for the weaknesses.

Many dyslexic children describe visual difficulties – the print blurring and letters jumping. They skip lines and miss out words, but have perfect eyesight. Their immature visual system may not be causing the dyslexia, but if there is a reading difficulty anyway, the least the child should expect is to be able to see the print clearly!

Many dyslexic children find background noise confusing, find it hard to take in a list of instructions, confuse similar sounding words and are sensitive to loud noise – but they can hear well. Their immature auditory system may not be the cause of the dyslexia, but wouldn't it make life easier if they could hear more accurately and process more quickly?

Many dyslexic children have poor handwriting – their hand aches, they have an unusual or tense pencil grip, they write too slowly and the results don't reflect the effort that has gone into the work. Their immature motor system may not be the cause of the dyslexia but wouldn't it be nice if their hands didn't hurt so much and the writing could flow smoothly?

Many dyslexic children are disorganised, easily distracted, find sport difficult, can't sit still, find it hard to concentrate, and get angry or upset. Life can be very exhausting for them.

All these difficulties reflect early developmental delay during the period when the central nervous system is initially developing – hence the global nature of the problems.

If this developmental delay is rectified and the foundations strengthened, the next developmental stage can begin, which is training these systems to obey our orders and automatically perform the increasingly complicated tasks we set them. Practice makes perfect and any other training given by the specialists in each area can then be even more effective and worthwhile.

If we look at the three main difficulties already described (and there are many more) the NDD involvement can be explained more fully.

THE VISUAL SYSTEM

The visual system is directly linked to the balance system. It is much easier to stand on one leg with the eyes open than closed. The balance mechanism is the first system to be fully developed in the human and is a major foundation stone for later development. If the balance mechanisms are immature, so the visual system will be also, because of their direct connection. Balance is known to be a major factor in dyslexia as, in addition to its foundational role, it acts as our internal compass giving us our sense of self in space, direction and orientation, quite apart from keeping us upright!

THE AUDITORY SYSTEM

The auditory system begins to develop very early in life. If it remains immature for any reason, it can mean that our pattern of hearing is not smooth. Some sounds come through louder than others – drowning out the softer sounds and distorting the message; an 'a' may be perceived as an 'e' for instance.

Another sign of immaturity is left ear dominance – very common in dyslexic children. Our language-processing areas are in the left-hand side of the brain with right ear dominance; speech travels across and directly into these centres. Left ear dominance; causes it to travel to the right hemisphere where it has to cross back into the left. The sound, therefore, travels twice as far and takes twice as long to get there. The child gets left behind and cannot follow a list of instructions.

HANDWRITING

When a small baby turns its head to the side – he is developmentally programmed to straighten the arm on the side he is facing. If this stage is not thoroughly worked through and this reflex does not completely disappear ready for the next stage, then when a child starts school he cannot comfortably keep the facing arm bent across the midline. Writing cannot become a natural, easy, subconscious activity for him.

Practice also makes perfect for these early developmental stages. By going back and constantly repeating these baby movements, no matter how old we really are, we can do the job again, and this time get it right – moving gradually from stage to stage until the whole system is more mature.

The Role of the Neuro-Developmental Therapist

Neuro-developmental therapists (NDTs) are trained to assess overall central nervous system functioning. They look at:

- cross muscle co-ordination
- fine motor skills

- balance

- patterns of motor development

- cerebellar functioning

- laterality

- oculo-motor functioning

- visual perceptual abilities

- hand/eye co-ordination

- auditory functioning

- reflexes.

This gives therapists a full picture of which areas have not been perfected in the first place and enables them to tailor an individual movement programme for each child which will fill in these gaps and mature overall functioning. These exercises, which replicate early developmental movements, are done at home and take only five to ten minutes a day. Progress is checked approximately every two months, and the programme changes as and when necessary. It usually takes between a year and 18 months to complete the process – never to be repeated.

As these early movement patterns are corrected, so the central nervous system matures and all the above difficulties improve. A child is then in a much stronger position to benefit from the training and educational input needed to catch up.

For further information contact the Developmental Practitioners Association.

CHAPTER 7

Chiropractic and Dyslexia
by Dr Chris Vickers

Chiropractic is defined as being the science and art of detecting and correcting dysfunctional areas (known in the jargon as subluxations) of the pelvis, spine and skull (cranium) which cause interference in the normal functioning of the nervous system, which these structures either house, support or protect.

As the nervous system is the organiser and regulator of all bodily functions, it has become well known within the profession, and by patients who have received treatment from chiropractors, that correction of these dysfunctional areas can have far-reaching positive effects on many areas of the body. It is because of this interconnectedness that practitioners and patients alike have in the past reported beneficial effects with dyslexia and dyspraxia problems, purely as a spin-off from correction of other areas relating to a particular symptom which a person has presented.

Chiropractic originated in the USA in 1895 with a magnetic healer called Palmer correcting a misaligned vertebra in the spine of a local janitor. This had the effect of curing the deafness he had experienced in one ear for the previous 17 years. Despite opposition from medical authorities, the profession has developed into being the third largest primary health care provider in the Western world after medicine and dentistry.

At a similar time, also in the United States, osteopathy was developing along similar lines. Osteopaths, however, believed that spinal and pelvic dysfunction disturbed blood flow rather than nerve function. In the early part of the 1900s a man named De Jarnette was injured in a factory explosion and sought treatment from an early osteopath named Andrew Still, who later became the founder of cranial osteopathy. He helped De Jarnette and encouraged him to become an osteopath; this he did, and soon afterwards also qualified as a chiropractor.

At this time cranial osteopaths were having great results with Still's techniques but were also noticing some adverse reactions, which were unexpected. De Jarnette discovered a method by which he could reproducibly correct pelvic dysfunction, which simultaneously minimised the frequency of adverse reactions to cranial corrections. He developed his research over many years into a very well known and widely practised chiropractic technique, by the name of sacro-occipital technique (SOT), which highlighted the functional relationship between pelvis and cranium.

Many chiropractors and osteopaths have studied cranial dysfunction and correction intensively. Through clinical observation it was noticed that practitioners who specialised in cranial work were often able to give positive help to people (especially children) with learning and behavioural difficulties. At first this was difficult to quantify and predict. After careful study and organisation this work has developed significantly from De Jarnette and Still's work.

The art and science of muscle testing (known as applied kinesiology) was developed by a chiropractor called Goodheart, also in the USA. His methods helped evaluate cranial problems and along with SOT and other chiropractic techniques has advanced the study of cranial dysfunction with regard to correcting dyslexic and dyspraxic problems.

It is now understood that proper eye function is of major significance in learning, as well as in the efficient delivery of the sensory ocular (eye) information to the visual centre of the brain and the distribution of this information either into motor function (i.e. performing and action) or sensory assimilation (i.e. comprehension, imagination or memory).

If a person has cranial (or indeed spinal or pelvic) dysfunction, then interference can occur both directly to cranial nerves, most especially to the third (oculomotor) cranial nerve, which regulates eye muscle movements, and indirectly to the correct assimilation and mental processing of sensory eye information. Either or both of these can result in inappropriate eye movements (which may reduce reading speed or effectiveness owing to alteration of normal eye scanning) or can alter the processing of information into the brain, thereby possibly interfering with understanding and memory mechanisms. This may be due to faulty function of the second (optic) cranial nerve or poor cross-over of the information into both sides of the brain.

Correction of faulty pelvic, spinal or cranial mechanics can alter the functioning of the membranes (sheaths) that surround the spinal cord and brain. It is believed that incorrect balance between these membranes has both a direct and indirect influence upon the electrical functioning of the brain. The chiropractic sacro-occipital cranial and muscle testing (AK) techniques make the most of these connections for both identifying and correcting problems. The corrections are very gentle and may involve soothing light moulding of the skull bones, or placing special blocks under the pelvis while encouraging certain breathing patterns.

Another chiropractor, named Ferreri, again from the USA, developed a system of muscle testing for various nerve circuits in the body known as reflexes that are concerned with the four primal survival systems in humans – feeding, fight/flight, reproduction and the immune systems. He noted that all bodily functions must work within or through these survival systems in an organised and integrated manner. Various forms of stress including physical, emotional, chemical or environmental trauma can and do interfere with the organised function of these reflex systems.

The technique he founded, Neural Organisation Technique (NOT) was a synthesis of muscle testing (AK), SOT and cranial testing. Early in its development the organisational effect of NOT on the nervous system was recognised as helping people with dyslexia and learning difficulties. A specific deficit in the vestibular-ocular reflex system (connecting balance and vision) was found to be present in this condition. Accordingly many chiropractors and then kinesiologists became interested in learning how to address these and other conditions which have resisted the best efforts of orthodox treatment.

As a result of NOT work, which involves stimulating reflex areas on the body in a specific sequence, often with the person changing eye function as directed (i.e. eyes open/closed), it was also noted that many other conditions were helped along with the frequently identified ADD (attention deficit disorder and ADHD (attention deficit hyperactive disorder), which often require more extensive treatment protocols. These reflex stimulations are thought to clear dysfunctional nerve programmes in the spinal cord and brain. No drugs are ever used in the correction of these conditions.

Chiropractors and osteopaths who have developed an interest in this type of work have shown that various exercises are frequently helpful in assisting corrections, as well as maintaining the gains made and preventing relapse. These may be eye exercises or hand-eye co-ordination exercises. However, it has been found that unless these structural (pelvic/spinal/cranial) or reflex faults are corrected, the individual is most unlikely to improve by performing corrective exercises alone. Dietary advice is commonly found to be necessary – the encouragement to take in the correct type of essential fatty acids which help improve nerve function, to eat plenty of raw fruits and vegetables and drink plenty of water.

Correction of these conditions is best undertaken by a team approach with good communications between team members. The team is likely, but not exclusively, to contain an educational psychologist, an optician, a nutritionist and a properly qualified chiropractor/osteopath. It should go without saying that these team members should be in regular contact with the patient, parents and schoolteachers (if applicable), as well as with each other; they should all have a specific interest in this area of work as a prerequisite to being involved.

For further information contact the British Chiropractic Association.

CHAPTER 8

Vitamins and Minerals

Most people would accept the premise that eating a balanced diet is essential to our children's mental and physical development. Many scientific studies have shown that a nutritionally complete diet is necessary in the development of vision, learning ability and co-ordination. But are our children getting a well balanced diet, or should they be taking supplements? Can taking supplements of fatty acids, zinc or iron 'cure' dyslexia? Many parents who use these tablets say a resounding 'yes', and there now appears to be strong evidence to support this.

One study indicated that children who had a decent breakfast before exams performed much better than those who skipped breakfast or just had a bowl or cereal. The most likely reason for this is that the breakfast provides a short-lived surge in blood glucose levels, thereby improving brain functioning within a short period of time.

Fatty Acids and Efalex

Lack of any vitamin will cause problems, but Dr Jacqueline Stordy, a former senior lecturer at Surrey University, noticed that dyslexia appeared to be more prevalent in people who had not been breastfed. Breast milk contains fatty acids that are known to be important in helping to maintain eye and brain function, and her research found people with dyslexia had a deficiency in this area. Other studies have concluded that abnormal levels of fatty acids in the brain could result in the practical and behavioural problems experienced by dyslexic children as well as those with dyspraxia and ADHD.

Efalex is a supplement that contains fatty acids, evening primrose oil, tuna oil, thyme oil and vitamin E. The manufacturers of Efalex state:

> Essential fatty acids play a vital role in maintaining the eye and brain function, so it is important to get sufficient from our diet to satisfy the body's needs. Learning ability in humans begins to show itself early in childhood. Some parents discover that although their children are intelligent and creative, they can find everyday tasks daunting, and some children may even demonstrate unruly or disruptive behaviour. Scientific research has shown that a nutritionally complete diet that includes certain fatty acids can play a vital part in the development of vision, learning ability and co-ordination.

Michael – 9 years

Michael has dyslexia and ADHD. He had severe literacy problems and found it difficult to concentrate and sit still for long.

Michael attended the Swindon Dyslexia Centre twice each week to help him with his problems. Whilst there his mother read an article on Efalex. She said she was desperate and 'willing to try anything'. Within weeks of Michael taking the tablets, she noticed a difference in his behaviour at home. The school also commented on his improvement in concentration span and behaviour. Michael is now making steady progress with reading, writing and spelling and can sit still for much longer periods.

His mother said: 'It is truly remarkable, certainly worth the money.'

Many parents attending the Swindon Dyslexia Centre whose children have taken Efalex, say that within a very short period of time their child is calmer, can concentrate better and has started to catch up with his reading and writing. This does not appear to help everyone but it is certainly worth trying.

Efalex is manufactured by Efamol and is available in capsule or liquid form (about £8.00 buys 56 capsules or a 150ml bottle), from most chemists and supermarkets.

Iron Supplements

Research appears to show that anaemia affects the mental abilities of children. Animal research has also hinted that iron deficiency is enough to change brain iron levels, which in turn alters the way neurotransmitters behave in the brain.

Zinc Supplements

Zinc is one of our body's most important trace minerals. Research has shown that people with dyslexia have been linked to a deficiency of this mineral.

Zinc plays an important part in the body's immune system. A shortage can affect the healing process because the body is unable to store it, therefore it is vital that we eat enough daily to stay healthy. An indicator of a lack of zinc includes white marks on fingernails and dandruff. Zinc can be found in many foods including:

- lean meat
- liver
- cheese
- chicken
- eggs
- wholemeal breads

- wholegrain cereals

- dried beans

- seafood.

Zinc can be destroyed or blocked by various things, including tannin (found in tea, coffee and alcohol), food colourings and additives.

Dr Ellen Grant, Kingston-upon-Thames, was an adviser to the Dyslexic Institute for over 20 years. She stated in her book *Sexual Chemistry – Understanding Our Hormones*: 'Virtually all the dyslexic children we have tested are short of zinc, and children who are hyperactive with behaviour problems often turn out to be zinc deficient.' No further research appears to have been done on this.

Summary

Most people agree that if we eat a well-balanced diet there is no need to take supplements and our children will be healthy and well. However, that is not always possible when we are rushing around trying to be all things to everyone, grabbing frozen meals and take-away meals.

There is plenty of research that indicates some children are lacking in fatty acids, iron and zinc, yet these vitamins and minerals are vital to maintain the health of our children. Whilst there appears to be a lot of research into fatty acids, unfortunately, although Grant appears to have identified a major problem with zinc deficiency, little research seems to have been done on this.

According to the media and some parents, dyslexic children are making 'miraculous' progress after taking supplements – as parents, ultimately, the decision has to be left to you.

CHAPTER 9

Multi-Sensory Teaching Methods

What is Multi-sensory?

Specialists in education acknowledge that the most successful way of teaching is by using a structured multi-sensory approach. This is the quickest way for all students to learn and is particularly relevant for students with learning difficulties.

Multi-sensory means using the different senses:

- auditory

- visual

- oral

- kinaesthetic.

The teaching methods and practice require the simultaneous interaction of the sensory channels. An example of this can be seen using alphabet wooden letters where students:

1. *listen* to the teacher saying the sound of the letter

2. *look* at the letter

3. *repeat* the letter sound to the teacher and

4. *trace a finger* over the outline of the letter

Another example uses a tray of sand or salt:

1. *listen* to the teacher saying the sound of the letter

2. *look* at the letter the teacher writes on the blackboard

3. *repeat* the letter sound to the teacher and

4. *write* the letter in the sand.

Using this integrated multi-sensory approach, combined with memory, perceptual training and regular over-learning activities, students achieve success by ensuring permanent automatic responses are built up through the different activities. Each student should follow a carefully structured, individual programme designed to overcome his difficulties and provide a sound basis for future study.

Teaching Schemes

There are many well-established successful teaching schemes available as well as a wide range of educational games and computer-based learning programmes, including:

- Alpha to Omega

- ARROW

- Hickey Multi-Sensory Language Course

- Multi-Sensory Learning – StarSkills

- Units of Sound (Multimedia)

- WordShark

- NumberShark.

Alpha to Omega

Alpha to Omega was devised by a speech therapist with in-depth knowledge of phonetics and linguistics pertinent to the teaching of speech and language skills. It was the first complete teaching programme based on structured, sequential phonetic and linguistic concepts to be published in Britain. Along with the Hickey Multi-Sensory Language Course it is often seen as the Bible in teaching circles and has been added to and extended since it was first developed.

Alpha to Omega is available for teachers and activity workbooks, which can be photocopied, can be used for individual students or in a whole class setting.

Alpha to Omega is available from Heinemann Educational Books (see 'Useful Addresses').

ARROW

See Chapter 5 'Hearing'.

Hickey Multi-Sensory Language Course

This scheme was first published as the Kathleen Hickey Language Kit, and along with Alpha to Omega is one of the most highly respected teaching programmes available. 'Hickey' is a multi-sensory learning programme designed to prevent failure and to remedy disorders in reading, writing and spelling. Suitable for any age range from infants to adults, it can be used for individuals or small group teaching.

It is available from The Psychological Corporation (see 'Useful Addresses').

Multi-Sensory Learning – StarSkills

Multi-Sensory Learning – StarSkills has been developed based on the order of sounds presented in the Hickey course. It is suggested that this programme be read in conjunction with the Hickey course mentioned above. It is a complete manual with all necessary equipment for active education without hours of preparation and planning for teachers. The package includes worksheets, cards, tapes and games.

Multi-Sensory Learning – StarSkills is available from Multi-Sensory Learning (see 'Useful Addresses').

Units of Sound (Multimedia)

Units of Sound was developed by Walter Bramley of the Dyslexia Institute over 20 years ago. It was originally on audiocassette and has now been updated and put on to CD-ROM, thereby making it a multi-media programme. It has a strong phonic/sound element and each page focuses on a particular unit of sound, combined with a visual word approach. Units of Sound is a proven multi-sensory learning resource.

Units of Sound (Multimedia) is available at a cost of £259 from the Dyslexia Institute (see 'Useful Addresses').

WordShark and NumberShark

WordShark is a computer program covering the word recognition and spelling requirements of the National Literacy Strategy Framework for Teaching. Combining the excitement of computer games with learning, this program offers 26 different games that use sound, graphics and text to teach and reinforce word recognition and spellings. It is based on the Alpha to Omega Activity Pack, which closely follows the normal pattern of phonological acquisition with each stage leading naturally and logically to the next.

NumberShark combines motivation and enjoyment within a structured learning process. The program addresses many of the difficulties that lead students to dislike maths. It features 30 different games covering addition, subtraction, multiplication and division in ways that add meaning and understanding to these operations.

WordShark and NumberShark are published by White Space and are available at £50–£60 from AVP (see 'Useful Addresses').

CHAPTER 10

Can Computers Help?

Computers are now an important part of classroom teaching. No computer package can ever be a substitute for good teaching but the correct software packages can help and support the busy teacher. Many programs can be incorporated into a specialist teaching scheme.

Computers take the hard work out of learning – they make learning fun.

There is now a vast array of specialist software for people with learning difficulties. Computers can help in many different ways including:

- checking spellings and giving practice through reading instructions

- immediate reinforcement

- essential over-learning

- programs with speech make learning truly multi-sensory

- learning to use databases and spreadsheets may aid sequential thinking and problem-solving skills

- printouts are often easier to read than a child's own writing

- allowing students to make and self-correct mistakes in private

- ability to motivate students, being a truly multi-sensory, novel and stimulating way to learn.

The advantage of instant feedback, the possibility of echoing each letter name, each word, each sentence of any marked section of text, as well as reading through, helps the student with a poor short-term memory and ensures an efficient transfer to long-term memory – making learning fun. Software packages can provide structured learning to develop skills continuously, giving support for literacy and numeracy.

Software Packages

There are many software packages available but the following three are essential for the busy student, at school, college or in the office. A desktop publishing package is also useful.

Microsoft Word is an excellent word processing package that enables you to write letters, reports, etc., with the added advantage of a spell-checker and grammar checker. It is very easy to use. Students with learning difficulties say that when they use a word processor 'the written world opens up' to them – at last they can put their thoughts down on paper. Students may be able to use a word processor for coursework and exams.

Excel is a spreadsheet package that is an excellent program for showing students who are shy of figures that there is nothing to worry about. The graphs enhance and display the student's work in many different ways.

Access is a good database package. Databases can be difficult to use in the first instance but once mastered they are excellent for organising lists of friends, business acquaintances, homework and assignments.

One of the best software packages I have found is *Microsoft Office* which incorporates all of the above.

Other Useful Software

Mavis Beacon for Kids is an excellent touch-typing course for students of all ages. If students can find their way around a keyboard quickly this will help with all coursework and speed up their presentations.

Microsoft Publisher is a desktop publishing package that is very useful to display posters, newsletters, reports, brochures, etc.

The award-winning *IBM ViaVoice Gold* lets you speak to your computer at up to 140 words per minute with very high accuracy. It is a very good aid, and saves you all that typing!

TOUCH-SCREEN COMPUTERS

These computers work through the student simply touching the screen with his hands. They are useful in identifying and assessing children from four years of age for early signs of specific learning difficulties. Touch-screens are used in the driving theory test.

Specialist Software

There are many specialist software packages for dyslexics available today. However, one word of caution: some packages in shops are not always suitable for dyslexic students because the language used is not appropriate.

The British Dyslexia Association Computer Committee has been reviewing programs for dyslexia/specific learning difficulties for over 10 years. They have a series of booklets, which are updated frequently. My advice would be to use software that is recommended by them as it is already tried and tested.

For further information contact the British Dyslexia Association (see 'Useful Addresses').

Games

Arcade-type games, often seen as students just playing, can help develop hand/eye co-ordination and can be a fun approach adapted to make learning almost painless. Sinking battleships in alphabetical order is far more exiting than looking for X, Y, Z, etc, on a keyboard.

The Hands-free computer

Computers due to go on sale soon will have neither screen, keyboard nor mouse, and are controlled by hand movements in mid-air. The virtual computer will be introduced in offices and operating theatres. Hand movements will be picked up by cameras, coupled to pattern recognition software and used to control the computer in a similar way to a conventional mouse. Although these systems will at first cost over £1000 more than conventional personal computers, they will doubtless bring many benefits.

Computers and Examinations

Many schools allow children to use computers to complete GCSE coursework, and they may be allowed to use them for their exams. Students have argued for years that an exam is to test their knowledge, not their writing ability!

Dyslexic pupils may get special dispensation to use a computer in an examination. At the moment there does not appear to be a standard set of rules and the school or college has to request the information from the relevant examining board.

Psychometric Testing

Psychometric testing is benificial to all students, but it is expensive so some schools only use it for children with dyslexia or special needs.

Psychometric testing can be carried out in schools, colleges, universities, libraries and careers offices, in conjunction with the careers adviser. They are comprehensive paper and pencil tests and are usually simple 'tick the box' style. These tests provide an objective assessment of an individual's abilities and personality. They then match the information keyed in by the student with possible career choices held on a computer. After analysing the student's personal information and interests, they suggest career choices that the student may not have thought of.

There are many different types of tests around but they all work on the same principle.

CHAPTER II

Neuro-Linguistic Programming

Neuro-Linguistic Programming (NLP) was developed over 30 years ago by Dr Richard Bandler (a mathematician) and Dr John Grinder (a professor of linguistics). Dr Bandler and Dr Grinder wanted to symbolise the relationship between the brain, language and the body.

The theory tries to explain the way we process our thoughts to achieve a way of working. It involves:

BRAIN (NEURO)
LANGUAGE (LINGUISTIC)
BODY (PROGRAMMING)

Every baby is born programmed to learn, but what is it that makes some of us electricians, cooks or mathematicians? How does our brain make the distinction? NLP helps us to make the most of what we have and teaches us to reach our full potential by tapping into the way each and every one of us learns. We all think, learn and react differently to everyday situations.

In any learning situation, whether it is in school, college or at the workplace, all good teachers and tutors try to assess the way students learn, so they can adapt their teaching methods to suit the individual. This is easier said than done – it is sometimes very difficult to see how a person learns, when they do not know themselves.

One example of how people think differently can be seen if we look at students with dyslexia. It can be argued that dyslexic people think more and in greater depth than the average person. They use parallel, or lateral, thinking rather than the usual serial thinking, and often reach a solution without using a series of logical steps of serial thought. When a dyslexic student attempts a maths problem he will probably be able to reach the answer without being able to write down *how* he reached it (although he will be able to tell you). This can lead to his work being downgraded because teachers expect the 'working out' to be shown. Other students, if they understand the question, will have no problem showing exactly how they achieved the answer.

NLP and Dyslexia

Here is an extract from the Encyclopedia of Systemic NLP by Judith DeLozier and Robert Dilts.

> NLP approaches the treatment of dyslexia as being primarily an issue of developing and utilising the appropriate cognitive strategies and capabilities. The eye movements of dyslexic individuals, for example, tend to reflect their difficulties linking sound and images. When spelling, for instance, they will often look down and to the left (the accessing cue for internal dialogue) instead of up and to their left (the accessing cue for visual memory). NLP has had a high degree of success in helping people who have been diagnosed with dyslexia. In particular, the NLP Spelling Strategy (which teaches learners to form mental pictures of words) has been shown to improve the spelling ability of individuals with dyslexia, often quite dramatically.

> There are also issues of emotional frustration and limiting beliefs that arise as a result of the learning difficulties, negative feedback and labelling that people with dyslexia confront as part of their educational experience. These types of problems can be effectively dealt with through NLP techniques such as Change Personal History and Re-imprinting.

Steps of the NLP Visual Spelling Strategy

The functions described above may be put into the following simple step-by-step format:

1. Place the correct spelling of the word to be learned either:

    (a) directly in front of you at about eye level; or

    (b) above eye level and to your upper left (or right if you are left handed).

2. Close your eyes and think of something that feels confident, familiar and relaxing. When the feeling is strong, open your eyes and look at the correct spelling.

    (a) If you placed the correct spelling in front of you at eye level, move your eyes up and to the left (or right) and picture the correct spelling in your mind's eye.

    (b) If you placed the correct spelling to your upper left, remove the correct spelling, but keep your eyes up and to the left and continue to see the correct spelling in your mind's eye.

3. Look up at your mental image and verbalise (or write) the letters you see. Check what you have verbalised or written with the correct spelling. If any letters are missing or incorrect, return to step 1, and use the Helpful Hints to help clarify your mental image.

4. Look up at your mental image and spell the word backwards (i.e. verbalise or write the letters down from right to left). Compare what you have verbalised or written with the correct spelling. If you have difficulty or any letters are missing or if incorrect, go back to step 2 and use

the Helpful Hints to assist in clarifying your
mental image.

Helpful Hints

1. Picture the word in your favourite colour.

2. Make any unclear letters stand out by making
    them look different from the others in some way,
    e.g. bigger, brighter, closer, a different colour,
    etc.

3. Break the words into groups of three letters and
    build your picture three letters at a time.

4. Put the letters on a familiar background. Picture
    something like a familiar object or movie scene,
    then put the letters you want to remember on
    top of it.

5. If it is a long word, make the letters small
    enough so that you can see the whole word
    easily.

6. Trace the letters in the air with your finger and
    picture in your mind the letters you are wiring.

Today NLP is used in nearly every working environment in the
world. It can be adapted to meet different situations and environ-
ments. It finds out exactly how *you* learn and helps you to improve
these instincts – thereby reaching your full potential.

CHAPTER 12

Phono-graphix

Dr Diane McGuinness, a professor of psychology at South Florida University, developed the Phono-Graphix approach to reading. Her book *Why Children Can't Read* has become a valuable educational tool in America. Her son Geoffrey and his wife Carmen have continued to develop her work. Their programme is so successful that they now have Phono-Graphix centres in many countries of the world, including Britain.

Phono-Graphix, as its name suggests, is a phonics-based reading system that starts with the sounds of the language and letters. The teacher says each sound first and the child replicates this – as he hears it. The Phono-Graphix method teaches children that groups of letters are sounds. English is broken down into 134 of these sounds in groups of from one to four letters. The teacher shows the child a picture of an object, such as a dog. The child says the word for the picture and listens for the first sound 'd'. This continues until all 134 sounds are learnt. Once students can identify the sounds of letters they can work on the more complex words.

The children usually attend a 12-hour teaching programme, as Geoffrey and Carmen McGuinness believe this is the optimum amount of time required to teach a child to read.

As of September 1999 over 5000 people have been trained and certified in Phono-Graphix worldwide; over 1000 of these teachers are in Britain.

Although phonics is used in Britain, children learn sounds, such as a, b and c. The Phono-Graphix method appears to be successful because children are taught that words are sound pictures of the language they already have. For example 'cow' is not pronounced 'c' 'o' 'w' but divided into the sounds 'c' and 'ow'. It is this different approach to phonics using Phono-Graphix that appears to be successful with dyslexic students. A scheme is operating in Britain piloting the Phono-Graphix method in schools and local education authorities around the country, including East Basildon, Manchester, Rutland, Leicester and Bristol.

Articles on Phono-Graphix first appeared in British newspapers in May 1998 and were met with a storm of interest. The McGuinnesses have hosted several UK conferences and talks, and have appeared on BBC television. They have also had several books published.

The programme costs approximately £30 per hour. Or if you would like to combine the course with a holiday to America, the Orlando Clinic in Florida, offers a one-week intensive course from Monday to Friday for three hours a day which is approximately $535.

For further information contact Phono-Graphix (see 'Useful Addresses').

CHAPTER 13

The Value of Play

Dyslexia, dyspraxia and attention deficit/hyperactivity disorder (AD/HD) appear to be more prevalent today. Is it because we do not play with our children the way that our parents did?

When we talk about playing, most people will reach for board games, computer programs and the like, yet playing – make believe, kicking a ball, skipping and marbles – can do so much more. Do you know how many skills are developed playing these games? More importantly, these games are free or cost a few pence – yet the skill gains are enormous.

Playing fulfils lots of different necessities. First and foremost it *amuses* children and second it *aids their development*. Little did my parents know when they played games with us like I-spy or What's the time Mr Wolf? that they were helping to develop our listening and language skills, memory and co-ordination. When we were singing nursery rhymes they didn't realise that at the time we were developing a sense of sequencing, memory and auditory skills as well as rhythm.

Is it because we have always taken these things for granted and that most of these games are free, that we sometimes overlook them today?

I have listed just a few of the different games that will help enrich your child's language and development. Children love these games because first and foremost they are *playing* with you and perhaps more importantly from a parent's point of view, they are *learning*. Some of these games can take a few minutes – but rest assured every one of them will help your child's development.

I Went to the Market

Sequential memory, auditory memory and vocabulary

I went to market and bought some ... Apples, Bananas, Carrots, etc.

Each person takes it in turn to add an item in alphabetical order. For example:

Parent says: 'I went to the market and bought an Apple'

Child says: 'I went to the market and bought an Apple and Banana'

Parent says: 'I went to the market and bought an Apple, Banana and Carrots'

The Parson's Cat

Sequential memory, auditory memory and vocabulary

Parent says: 'The Parson's cat is an Affectionate cat.'

Child says: 'The Parson's cat is an Affectionate, Black cat.'

Parent says: 'The Parson's cat is an Affectionate, Black, Cuddly cat.'

As before, each person takes it in turn to add an item in alphabetical order.

Whip & Top

Co-ordination

To play this game you need a whip and a top. The top is a small, usually wooden, top with grooves in it. The whip can be made of anything, but is usually made from something similar to a leather bootlace with a knot tied at the end of it. The game is played by hitting the top with the whip. The idea is to keep it spinning as long as possible. Just before it stops hit it again.

Fivestones/Jack

Co-ordination

This game is played using a 'jack' (any small object) and five or six little balls or stones. Throw the jack in the air and pick up as many balls or stones as you can before the jack falls to the ground. This can be played on your own or in competition with another person.

Kim's Game (A)

Observation and Memory

a) Place ten items on a tray.
b) Let the child look at them for a minute.
c) Cover with a cloth.
d) Ask the child to try to remember what was on the tray.

For very young children, use only five items and increase the number as they develop their memory skills.

Kim's Game (B)

Observation and Memory

a) Place several items on a tray.

b) Let the child look at them for a minute.

c) Ask the child to close his eyes.

d) Discreetly take one item away.

e) Can the child guess which item you have taken?

I-Spy

Listening, vocabulary, observation and rhyming

If you are in the car and you see a tree:

Parent says: 'I spy with my little eye something beginning with T'. Child looks around to see what begins with T. They can guess as many times as they like.

Sometimes, a problem can arise with this game because your child may be processing sounds differently from you. For instance a child may say 'c' for see-saw, but that is exactly why this game is so good.

Another version to develop rhyming skills is:

Parent says:'I spy with my little eye something rhyming with rat.' Child looks around to see what rhymes with rat.

Marbles

Co-ordination, visual and number skills

Lots of different games can be played with marbles and every once in a while they come back into fashion.

What's the Time Mr Wolf?

Listening, memory, rhythm and time

Children take it in turns to be the wolf. The children get in a row about ten feet behind the wolf.

Children: 'What's the time Mr Wolf?'
Wolf: 'One o'clock.'
Children: Take one step closer and repeat 'What's the time Mr Wolf?'
Wolf: 'Two o'clock'

Children take one step closer and repeat: 'What's the time Mr Wolf?'

Wolf: 'Three o'clock.'

and so on ... until Wolf shouts 'Dinnertime!'

At this point the wolf turns around and chases the children to catch one for his supper. The child he catches is then the wolf and the game is repeated.

Nursery Rhymes

Rhyme, rhythm, memory, sequencing, days of the week and numbers

There are many different nursery rhymes. All encourage children to sing along. They develop a sense of rhyme, rhythm and sequencing. Some, like *Solomon Grundy* and *Monday's Child*, also help to develop sequencing of days of the week.

Simon Says

Listening and co-ordination

Parent says: 'Simon says put your hand on your nose,' '…put your hand on your head,' '…hop,' '…jump,' etc.

You can progress as quickly as the child is able.

Kinaesthetic Awareness (Touching)

Touch, letters and numbers

Get a bag and put wooden letters or numbers inside. The child has to feel the letter and say what it is. This is a lot harder than you first think.

You can buy these letters with sand or felt on them.

Skipping

Co-ordination, rhyme, rhythm, vocabulary, memory and colours

Many of the skipping games that used to be played were excellent for developing co-ordination. Some games that were played with several children, chanting songs whilst they played, also developed memory skills and colour sense.

Dominoes

Visual sequencing, number and observation

People take it in turn to put the dominoes down and to keep the number or picture flowing.

Jigsaw Puzzles

Visual skills and co-ordination

Jenga

Co-ordination

For those who do not know this game, you don't know what you're missing. This is a wonderful game for all the family and can be particularly entertaining after a dinner party. It is one of the funniest games I know for developing co-ordination.

The game uses approximately 100 little blocks of wood. You build them into a tower and take it in turns to take a block out – without making the tower fall over.

Board Games

Co-ordination and memory skills

There are many good board games, which give excellent practice for various co-ordination and memory skills. These include the old favourites – Scrabble, Monopoly, Snakes & Ladders, Ludo and Draughts.

Physical Sports

Co-ordination and rhythm

We should not forget that a very important part of playing is physical sports which all develop co-ordination and social skills. Football, rugby, rounders, hockey, netball, etc., are all excellent.

Three Dimensional Games

Visuospatial skills and mathematical skills

Commercially available games include Othello, Master Mind, Connect 4, Rubik's Cube and Shut the Box.

Card games

Visual memory, arithmetic

There are many different card games such as snap, which can be used with pictures as well as numbers.

A very good way of learning multiplication tables is by using cards. First take out the Jack, Queen and King. Select the No. 2 card and place on the left-hand side. Put down the rest of the cards, and turn them over one at a time – multiplying each card by the No. 2. Once you have mastered the 2 times table, repeat these instructions using the No. 3 card, and so on.

SKILLS INVOLVED

Auditory Memory

I Went to the Market
The Parson's Cat
I-Spy
Nursery rhymes
What's the Time Mr Wolf?
Simon Says
Skipping

Sequential Memory

I Went to the Market
The Parson's Cat
Nursery rhymes
Dominoes

Vocabulary Extension

I-Spy
I Went to the Market
The Parson's Cat
Nursery rhymes
Skipping
Most board games

Observational Skills

Kim's Games
I-Spy
Dominoes
Most board games

Co-ordination

Whip & Top
Fivestones/Jacks
Jenga
All physical contact sport
Jigsaw puzzles
Marbles
Skipping
Simon Says

Visual Memory

Kim's Games
I-Spy
Dominoes
Most board games
Card games

Reading and Spelling

Most board games

Rhyme and Rhythm

I-Spy
What's the Time Mr Wolf?
Nursery rhymes
Skipping

Conclusion

I have given you many different options; which one you choose may very much depend on the individual concerned – and your purse strings. Many of these things are relatively new, some are old hat but just as useful. Certainly you need to keep an open mind when trying some of the strategies.

Early identification has to be the key, because once you identify a child as having a learning difficulty and rule out any medical problems, you can start working towards a solution.

I believe that the major advances in dyslexia will be made in the areas of genetics and diet. Whilst a lot of research is being carried out at the moment with genetics, I was amazed to find out that research had been carried out over 12 years ago which indicated that virtually all dyslexic children tested were zinc deficient. This now seems to be a forgotten fact! As a mother of two dyslexic children, I would like to know why this is so. If something simple like a vitamin supplement can solve dyslexic problems why hasn't more research been done to investigate this?

Since I have been working with dyslexics, I can say I have truly seen some 'miracle cures'. A parent was once overheard to say: 'I was desperate for help, I tried everything going. If someone had told me to stand on my head in a field in Leicester and it would cure my son's dyslexia – I would have done so.' I am sure you will agree that with the choice available in this book that won't be necessary.

I wish you all the very best and hope that you will all find your very own 'miracle cure'.

I'm Not Marking This Mess

I can see his face ready to blow
he shouts so the whole class will know
'Sir, Sir I'm stuck, I need more time.'
'I told you what to do, don't step out of line.'
I find it hard and embarrassing with him yelling
about my reading, writing and spelling.
'Hurry up, get on with it, I'm not marking this mess.'
I say, 'I need more time, I'm doing my best.'
He tells me little kids can do better than me
'I've seen better from my daughter, she's only three
where's your full stops and capital letters?
now go and sit down until you do better.'
It's hard to do my work I find
I never rest, it's always on my mind
then I get frustrated, rude and angry
because, he doesn't understand me.

By Mark Chivers
September 1995
Reprinted by kind permission of Forward Press.

Dyslexia A₂Z

Dyslexia A$_2$Z was founded to enable anyone with an interest in Dyslexia to find out information quickly and easily.

Dyslexia A$_2$Z (http://www.dyslexiaa2z.com)

Dyslexia A$_2$Z has information on the following:

Dyslexia Tutors

Psychologists

Dyslexia Assessments and Tests

Irlen Syndrome

Intuitive Colorimeter

Efalex

Books on Dyslexia

Specialist Software

ChromaGen

Phono-Graphix

Neuro-Linguistic Programming (NLP)

Neuro-Developmental Delay (NDD)

ARROW

and more …

Further Reading

Augur, J. (1995) *This Book Doesn't Make Sense.* Bath: Better Books and Software Ltd.

Beaver, D. (1998) *NLP for Lazy Learning: Making the Most of the Brains You Were Born With.* Shaftesbury, Dorset: Element Books.

Blackerby, D. (1996) *Rediscover the Joy of Learning.* Oklahoma City, OK: Success Skills.

Chivers, M. (ed) (1996) *Dyslexia: The Inner Hurt.* Forward Press.

Chivers, M.(1997) *A Parents Guide to Dyslexia and Other Learning Difficulties.* Peterborough: Need 2 Know.

Davis, R., Ronald, D. and Braun E. (1997) *The Gift of Dyslexia.* London: Souvenir Press Ltd.

Department for Education (1994) *Code of Practice on the Identification and Assessment of Special Educational Needs.* London: HMSO.

Dilts, R. (1996) *Visionary Leadership.* Meta.

Dilts, R. and Epstein, T. (1995) *Dynamic Learning.* Meta.

Doyle, J. (1995) *Dyslexia: An Introductory Guide.* London: Whurr.

Heaton, P. and Winterson, P. (1996) *Dealing with Dyslexia.* London: Whurr.

McGuiness, C. and McGuiness, G. (1998) *Reading Reflex.* Harmondsworth: Penguin.

McGuiness, D. (1997) *Why Children Can't Read.* Harmondsworth: Penguin.

McLoughlin, D., Fitzgibbon, G. and Young V. (1993) *Adult Dyslexia: Assessment, Counselling and Training.* London: Whurr.

Miles, T.R. and Miles, E. (1999) *Dyslexia a Hundred Years On.* Buckingham: Open University Press.

Ostler, C. (1999) *Dyslexia: A Parents' Survival Guide.* Ammonite Books.

Reid, G. (1998) *Dyslexia: A Practitioners Handbook.* Chichester: Wiley.

Snowling, M. and Stackhouse, J. (eds) (1996) *Dyslexia, Speech and Language: A Practitioner's Handbook.* London: Whurr.

Useful Addresses

ARROW (for help for students)
PO Box 71
Burnham-on-Sea TA9 3YS
Tel/Fax 01278 788 388
E-mail: goarrow@self-voice.co.uk
Website: http://www.self-voice.co.uk

The Arrow Trust (for training for teachers)
Bridgwater College
Bath Road
Bridgwater TA6 4PZ
Tel/Fax: 01278 441 249
E-mail: goarrow@self-voice.co.uk
Website: http://www.self-voice.co.uk

AVP
School Hill Centre
Chepstow
Gwent NP6 5PH
Tel: 01291 625 439
Fax: 01291 629 671
E-mail: info@avp.uk

British Chiropractic Association
29 Whitley Street
Reading RG2 0EG
Tel: 01734 757 557

British Dyslexia Association
98 London Road
Reading RG1 5AU
Tel: 0118 966 8271 (Helpline)
Tel: 0118 966 2677 (Administration)
Fax: 0118 935 1927
E-mail: info@dyslexiahelp-bda.demon.co.uk (Helpline)
E-mail: admin@bda-dyslexia.demon.co.uk (Administration)
Website: http://www.bda-dyslexia.org.uk/

Cerium Visual Technologies Ltd
Cerium Technology Park
Tenterden
Kent TN30 7DE
Tel: 01580 765211
Fax: 01580 765573
E-mail: admin@ceriumvistech.co.uk

Developmental Practitioners Association
PO Box 4567
Henley-on-Thames
Oxfordshire RG9 6XZ

Dyslexia Institute
133 Gresham Road
Staines
Middlesex TW18 2AJ
Tel: 01784 463 851
Fax 01784 460 747
E-mail: infor@dyslexia-inst.or.uk
Website: http://www.dyslexia-inst.org.uk

Educational Kinesiology Foundation
12 Golders Rise
Hendon
London NW4 2HR
Tel: 020-8202 9747
Fax: 020-8202 3890

Association of Educational Psychologists
3 Sunderland Road
Durham DH1 21H
Tel: 0191 384 9512
Fax: 0191 386 5287

Edward Marcus Ltd
Star House
High Street
Tideswell
Buxton
Derbyshire SK17 8LD
Tel: 01298 871 388
Fax: 01298 871 064
E-mail: lowvision@marcus.freeserve.co.uk
Website: http://www.marcus.freeserve.co.uk

Efamol Ltd
Weyvern House
Weyvern Park
Portsmouth Road
Peasmarsh
Guildford
Surrey GU3 1NA
Tel 0870 606 0128
Website: http://www.efamol.com

Heinemann Educational Books Ltd
Halley Court
Jordan Hill
Oxford OX2 8EJ
Tel: 01865 311 366

Helen Arkell Dyslexia Centre
Frensham
Farnham
Surrey GU10 3BW
Tel: 01252 792 400
Fax: 01252 795 669

Institute of Optometry
56 Newington Causeway
London SE1 6DS
Tel: 020 7407 4183

Keith Holland (Optometrist)
27 St George's Road
Cheltenham GL50 3DT
Tel: 01242 233 500
Fax: 01242 227 686
Website: http://www.keithholland.co.uk

LDA Living & Learning
Abbeygate House
East Road
Cambridge CB1 1DB
Tel: 01223 357 744
Fax: 01223 460 557
E-mail: ldaproddev@aol.com

Lucid Research Ltd

PO Box 63
Beverley
East Yorkshire HU17 8ZZ
Tel/Fax: 01482 465 589
Tel/Fax: 01482 465 589
Website: http://www.lucid-research.com

Multi-Sensory Learning

Earlstrees Court
Earlstrees Road
Corby
Northamptonshire NN17 4HH
Tel: 01536 399 003
Fax: 01536 399 012

NFER-Nelson

Delville House
2 Oxford Road East
Windsor
Berkshire SL4 1DF
Tel: 01753 858 961
Fax: 01753 856 830
E-mail: edu&hsc@nfer-nelson.co.uk
Website: http://www.nfer-nelson.co.uk

Phono-Graphix

PO Box 52
Harpenden
Hertfordshire AL5 22X
Tel: 0800 783 8824
Fax: 001 352 735 9294
Website: http://www.readamerica.net

Psychological Corporation
Harcourt Place
21 Jamestown Road
London NW1 1YA
Tel: 020 7424 4456
Fax: 020 7424 4457
E-mail: tpc@harcourt.com
Website: http://www.tpc-international.com

Royal National Institute for the Blind (RNIB)
224 Great Portland Street
London WIN 6AA
Tel: 020 7388 1266
Fax: 020 7388 2034
Website: http://www.rnib.org.uk

Royal National Institute for Deaf People
19 Featherstone Street
London EC1Y 8SL
Tel: 0870 605 0123 (Helpline)
Text: 0870 603 3007
Fax: 020 7296 8199
Website: http://www.rnid.org.uk

Scientific Learning
1995 University Avenue
Suite 4000
Berkeley
California 94704
Tel: 001 888 665 9707
Fax: 001 510 665 1717
E-mail: info@scilearn.com
Website: http://www.scientificlearning.com

Ultralase
The Chester Clinic
1 Vicars Lane
Chester CH1 1QX
Tel: 01244 403 030
Fax: 01244 350 316

The Contributors

Gail Saye is a neuro-developmental therapist and auditory training specialist practising near Devizes in Wiltshire. She has been working in this field for the past nine years and lectures to a variety of professionals and parents on the physical aspects of special learning difficulties. She is also a special needs governor at a local primary school and works in a voluntary capacity for the Independent Parent Support Service – helping parents through the process of getting special needs provision for their children. She is a founder member of the Developmental Practitioners Association – set up as an umbrella organisation for suitably trained and experienced professionals in a range of developmental disciplines. She has three children, one of whom is dyslexic.

Dr Colin Lane has extensive experience of teaching children and adults of all ages and abilities. His ARROW experience covers reception children to adults well into retirement age. He first began his work on ARROW self-voice teaching methods in 1974. From its innovative beginnings with special needs children, ARROW has been centred upon mainstream children and adults of all abilities. Dr Lane was awarded a Master's degree for his work on the improvement of speech and listening skills and was awarded a PhD from Exeter University for his work on ARROW self-voice. Dr Lane is the founder of The Arrow Trust, which trains teachers and assistants in the self-voice techniques.

Dr Keith Holland is an optometrist practising in Cheltenham, Gloucestershire, with a special interest in vision and learning. Over the last ten years he has built up one of the largest specialist practices in Europe, seeing children from 31 countries, dealing with the visual problems associated with dyslexia and learning difficulties. He has published many articles on the links between vision and literacy and lectures widely on the subject, both at home and abroad. He is the founder of the British Association of Behaviour Optometrists, a professional special interest group that represents practitioners around Britain working in this field.

Christopher Vickers chose chiropractic as a career after suffering a back injury at school. Conventional therapy had not worked, where chiropractic had. He graduated from the Anglo-European College of Chiropractic in 1981. Then he held an associateship in Edinburgh, followed by working in Zimbabwe and South Africa. On returning to the UK in 1986 he became involved in learning about cranial work, which he now teaches across Europe. During his work in this field he became increasingly interested in dyslexic problems and his interest was amplified by his having studied neural organisation technique (NOT). He now works in private practice in Cirencester.

Index